Mastering Forex: Unveiling Proven Strategies for Profitable Trading Success

SMART MONEY CONCEPT

THE ULTIMATE SMART MONEY TRADING CONCEPT

LENTLE ANDRIAS

CYNAUT

MASTERING FOREX: UNVEILING PROVEN STRATEGIES FOR PROFITABLE TRADING SUCCESS

THE ULTIMATE SMART MONEY TRADING CONCEPT
<<<<<?>>>>>

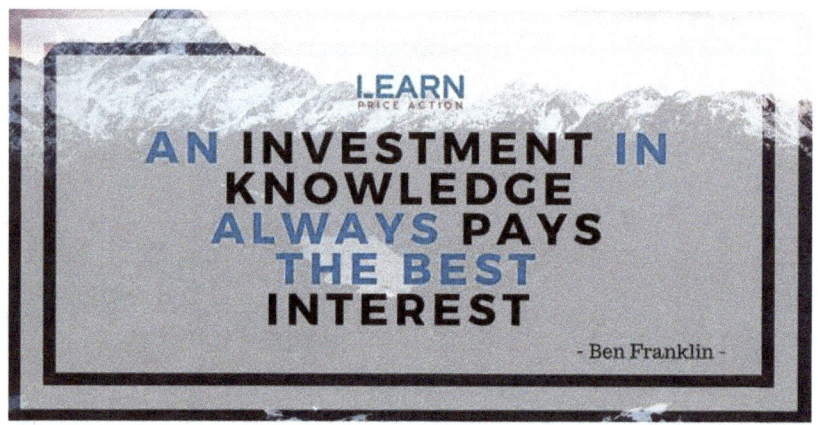

Cover design by Lentle Andrias
Image by macrovector on Freepik

ACKNOWLEDGMENTS

Writing a book is a journey that's made possible through the support, guidance, and encouragement of many individuals.

As the author of this book, I am grateful for the contributions and inspiration that have shaped its creation.

I extend my heartfelt gratitude to:

My Family: Your unwavering support and belief in my endeavors have been a constant source of motivation. Thank you for understanding the late nights and dedicated hours spent crafting this book.

Mentors and Traders: To those who have shared their wisdom and experience in the forex markets, your insights have been invaluable. Your guidance has enriched the content of this book and made it more relevant to aspiring traders.

Readers and the Trading Community: Your enthusiasm for learning and improving your trading skills is what drives authors like me to create valuable content. Your engagement and feedback have been instrumental in shaping the direction of this book.

Editorial and Publishing Teams: A big thank you to the professionals who helped refine the manuscript, ensuring that the content is clear, accurate, and reader-friendly. Your expertise has been a vital part of the publishing process.

Friends and Peers: Your encouragement, discussions, and brainstorming sessions have contributed to the depth and breadth of ideas presented in this book. Your diverse perspectives have added value beyond measure.

OpenAI and Research: The realm of forex trading is ever-evolving, and the insights and research provided by platforms like OpenAI have been instrumental in enhancing the quality of the content shared in this book.

Market Analysts and Experts: The work of market analysts and experts has provided a solid foundation for understanding the dynamics of the forex market. Their research and insights have been pivotal in shaping the content of this book.

To everyone who played a part, big or small, in bringing this book to life, your contributions have been acknowledged with gratitude. May the insights within these pages empower readers to navigate the forex trading landscape with confidence and skill.

With sincere appreciation,

LENTLE ANDRIAS

TRADING PLAN

1. **Trading Style and Strategy**.
2. **Personal Goals and Objectives**.
3. **Market Analysis**.
4. **Risk Management**
5. **Trade Execution**
6. **Psychology and Discipline**
7. **Record Keeping**
8. **Review and Improvement**
9. **Contingency Plans**
10. **Time Commitment**

RISK REWARD

*Use your stop loss as your entry signal.

***Risk Management-** A good risk-reward ratio is crucial for effective risk management. It helps you determine the amount of potential loss you're willing to accept for each trade relative to the potential gain.

***Assessing Trade Viability-** A higher ratio means that even if you have more losing trades than winning ones, you can still be profitable if your winning trades' rewards outweigh the losses..

***Maintaining Consistency-** Using a consistent risk-reward ratio can help you maintain a disciplined approach to trading. It prevents you from chasing after high-risk trades that might seem tempting but could lead to significant losses if they don't go as planned.

* **Adapting to Market Conditions:** Depending on market conditions, you might adjust your risk-reward ratio. In more volatile conditions, you might opt for a higher reward potential, while in less volatile conditions, you might accept a lower reward in exchange for a tighter stop-loss.

*Balancing Win Rate and Profitability:** A lower win rate can still lead to profitability if your risk-reward ratios are favorable. For instance, even if you win only 30% of your trades, if your average winning trade is two or three times larger than your average losing trade, you can still come out ahead.

PSYCHOLOGY IN FOREX

Navigating the Mindset for Success

Trading forex is not just a game of numbers and charts; it's a psychological battleground where emotions, discipline, and mindset play a pivotal role. Understanding and managing the psychological aspects of forex trading are essential for consistent success in the markets.

Emotional Roller Coaster

Forex trading is an emotional roller coaster. Fear and greed are two powerful emotions that can wreak havoc on even the most well devised trading strategies. Fear can lead to hesitation, causing missed opportunities or premature exits. Greed can result in overleveraging and taking unnecessary risks. Recognizing and controlling these emotions is paramount.

Discipline Amidst Chaos

Discipline is the cornerstone of successful trading psychology. Sticking to your trading plan, following risk management rules, and executing trades based on strategy rather than impulses are key components. Discipline keeps emotions in check and ensures that decisions are made logically, not emotionally.

Patience as a Virtue

In a world of instant gratification, patience is a rare and valuable trait in forex trading. Waiting for the right setups, not forcing trades, and allowing trades to play out according to plan require patience. Impatient traders often jump into trades prematurely or exit too early, missing out on potential profits.

Coping with Losses

Losses are inevitable in trading, but how you handle them defines your success. Accepting losses as a part of the game and learning from them is crucial. Avoid chasing losses or revenge trading, as they often lead to emotional decision-making and further losses.

Managing Success

Surprisingly, success can also be a psychological challenge. A string of winning trades might lead to overconfidence and deviation from your trading plan. It's essential to remain humble, stick to your strategies, and avoid becoming complacent.

Mind Over Market

Developing a strong mindset is like cultivating a mental edge over the market. Positive affirmations, visualization techniques, and maintaining a growth-oriented perspective can help you weather the storms and maintain focus during both winning and losing streaks.

Preventing Burnout

Trading can be intense and demanding. It's important to find a healthy balance between trading and other aspects of life to prevent burnout. Regular breaks, physical exercise, hobbies, and spending time with loved ones can recharge your mental batteries.

Continuous Learning

The forex market is ever evolving, and staying informed is essential. Continuous learning not only improves your trading skills but also keeps your mind engaged and adaptable to changing market conditions.

Seeking Support

Trading can be isolating, but it doesn't have to be. Engage with a community of traders, share experiences, and seek advice. Sometimes discussing challenges and successes with others can provide valuable perspectives and emotional support.

Conclusion

Trading forex is as much about understanding yourself as it is about understanding the markets. Developing a strong trading psychology takes time and effort, but it's a journey worth embarking on. By mastering your emotions, maintaining discipline, and fostering a resilient mindset, you can navigate the complex world of forex trading with confidence and achieve consistent success.

RULES FOLLOWED BY PROFESSINAL TRADERS

1. **Risk Management:**

    ◦ Never risk more than a certain percentage of your trading capital on a single trade.

    ◦ Use stop-loss orders to limit potential losses on each trade.

    ◦ Avoid overleveraging; keep position sizes in line

with your risk tolerance.

2. **Trading Plan:**

   ◦ Develop a detailed trading plan that outlines your goals, strategies, and approach to the markets.

   ◦ Stick to your trading plan and avoid impulsive decisions based on emotions.

3. **Discipline:**

   ◦ Follow your trading plan consistently, regardless of market conditions or emotions.

   ◦ Avoid chasing trades or making revenge trades after losses.

4. **Patience:**

   ◦ Wait for high-probability trade setups that align with your strategy.

   ◦ Avoid overtrading by only taking trades that meet your predefined criteria.

5. **Technical and Fundamental Analysis:**

   ◦ Conduct thorough analysis before entering a trade, using both technical and fundamental factors.

- Use technical indicators and chart patterns to identify potential entry and exit points.

6. **Trade Management:**

   - Let winners run by using trailing stop-loss orders or scaling out of positions gradually.
   - Cut losses quickly if a trade is not moving in your favor according to your analysis.

7. **Continuous Learning:**

   - Stay informed about market developments, news, and changes in economic indicators.
   - Keep refining your trading strategies based on new insights and experiences.

8. **Adaptability:**

   - Be flexible and willing to adjust your strategies based on changing market conditions.
   - Avoid becoming too attached to a single trading approach if it's not producing consistent results.

9. **Journaling and Analysis:**

   - Keep a trading journal to document your trades, including reasons for entry and exit, emotions, and outcomes.

- Regularly review your journal to identify patterns, strengths, and areas for improvement.

10. **Psychological Resilience:**

- Develop emotional resilience to handle both winning and losing streaks.

- Practice techniques like meditation or mindfulness to manage stress and emotions.

11. **Diversification:**

- Avoid concentrating your trading on a single instrument; diversify across different markets or currency pairs.

- Spread risk by having a variety of trading strategies that can perform in different market conditions.

12. **Long-Term Perspective:**

- Understand that trading is a marathon, not a sprint. Focus on consistent growth over time.

- Avoid making rash decisions based on short-term fluctuations.

Remember that these rules are not a one-size-fits-all solution. Professional traders often develop their own customized set of rules based on their individual experiences, risk tolerance, and trading style. It's important to develop rules that align with your strengths, preferences, and goals as a trader.

COMMON CHART PATTERNS

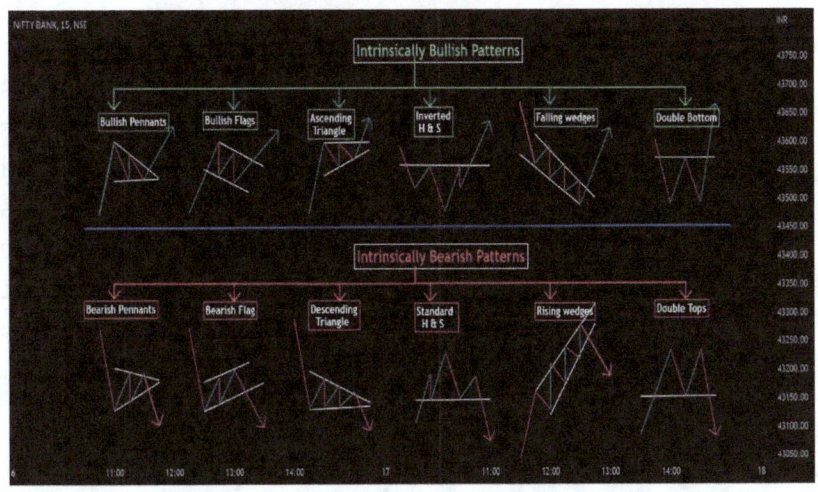

SMART MONEY CONCEPTS

INTRODUCTION

In the realm of financial markets, the concept of "**smart money**" holds a prominent place, acting as a guiding light for traders seeking an edge in their decision-making. Smart money refers to the capital controlled by sophisticated and well-informed investors who often possess insights, resources, and strategies beyond the average market participant. Understanding the nuances of smart money concepts unveils a deeper layer of market dynamics, providing a unique perspective for those looking to navigate the markets with finesse.

The Wisdom of Institutions and Professionals

Smart money, a term that resonates within the echelons of financial markets, finds its embodiment in institutional investors, hedge funds, and highly skilled professional traders. These entities are renowned for their unique position in the investment landscape, stemming from their intrinsic ability to harness an unparalleled understanding of market trends and dynamics. They represent a potent force, distinguished by their access to a vast reservoir of advanced research tools, substantial financial resources, and a depth of industry knowledge that few can rival.

Institutional investors, often comprising pension funds, endowments, and mutual funds, are entrusted with managing large pools of capital. They operate with a fiduciary responsibility to safeguard and grow the wealth of their stakeholders. This duty necessitates a profound understanding of the markets, which they achieve through rigorous analysis and research. Institutional investors deploy their resources strategically, diversifying across various asset classes, thereby serving as the cornerstone of the broader financial ecosystem.

Hedge funds, on the other hand, are renowned for their agility and flexibility. These investment vehicles, typically reserved for accredited investors, are known for their ability to employ a wide array of investment strategies, including long and short positions, derivatives, and alternative assets. Hedge funds are helmed by experienced portfolio managers who employ proprietary models and trading algorithms, aiming to deliver superior returns while effectively managing risk. Their ability to swiftly adapt to changing market conditions allows them to seize opportunities and mitigate threats, making them a dynamic force in the financial world.

Professional traders, including proprietary trading firms and seasoned individuals, are experts in the art of navigating financial markets. Armed with years of experience and in-depth knowledge, they employ a combination of technical and fundamental analysis to execute well-informed trades. Their proficiency in reading market sentiment, coupled with the latest technology and high-frequency trading strategies, enables them to capitalize on short-term price fluctuations. The impact of professional traders can be particularly felt in liquid markets, where their trading volumes can swiftly influence asset prices.

Collectively, these savvy market participants wield immense power. Their trading decisions and strategies resonate throughout the financial ecosystem, shaping the direction of asset prices, influencing market sentiment, and setting the tone for other market participants. It is not uncommon for their actions to trigger chain reactions, causing ripples that cascade through the markets, impacting individual investors, corporations, and even governments. As such, the activities of smart money are closely monitored and analyzed by investors worldwide, recognizing the profound impact they have on the intricate tapestry of global finance.

CONTRARIAN INSIGHTS: THE UNIQUE APPROACH OF SMART MONEY

A salient hallmark of smart money is its contrarian nature, setting it apart from the more conventional investment strategies often embraced by retail traders and novice investors. While the masses tend to follow the prevailing market sentiment and trends, smart money deliberately charts its own course by adopting a contrarian stance. This distinctive approach is anchored in a deep-seated belief that markets are not always rational and that investor behavior is subject to emotional highs and lows, leading to occasional mispricings and irrational exuberance.

When smart money adopts a contrarian strategy, it essentially positions itself against the prevailing market consensus. This approach is underpinned by a core philosophy that markets, in their collective wisdom, can be temporarily swayed by euphoria or fear, causing asset prices to deviate from their intrinsic values. Smart money, with its extensive resources and expertise, seeks to identify these disparities in valuation and exploit them to its advantage.

By actively taking positions that run counter to the popular sentiment, smart money effectively capitalizes on market mispricing. This willingness to swim against the current allows them to uncover investment opportunities that often remain concealed to those who simply follow the herd. They are adept at identifying inflection points in the market, whether it's recognizing a market bubble about to burst or spotting an undervalued asset ripe for a rebound.

Furthermore, the contrarian approach empowers smart money to manage risk more effectively. By not being swept away by the prevailing euphoria or fear-driven selling, they are less susceptible to the emotional roller coaster that can ensnare less experienced investors. Instead, they rely on thorough analysis, comprehensive research, and a disciplined approach to make informed decisions that stand the test of time.

In this manner, smart money plays a vital role in stabilizing markets and ensuring that asset prices align more closely with their intrinsic values over the long term. Their contrarian insights serve as a corrective force in the financial ecosystem, as they actively seek to address imbalances and correct market sentiment when it deviates from rationality.

In conclusion, the contrarian nature of smart money is not merely a quirk of their investment style; it is a fundamental tenet of their strategy. By challenging prevailing market sentiment and refusing to succumb to the allure of herd behavior, they forge a path to financial success that stands the test of time, allowing them to unlock hidden opportunities and, in the process, contribute to the overall stability and efficiency of financial markets.

MARKET MANIPULATION OR TRUE INSIGHT: THE COMPLEX WEB OF SMART MONEY'S INFLUENCE

The undeniable influence wielded by smart money within the financial arena often prompts the pressing question of whether their actions are motivated by market manipulation or rooted in genuine, insightful perspectives. This duality presents a multifaceted narrative that deserves closer scrutiny, as it underscores the fine line separating legitimate market insight from potentially unethical behavior.

Accusations of market manipulation have occasionally been directed towards institutional players, alleging that their massive financial clout enables them to orchestrate price movements to their advantage. These allegations can range from short-term tactics like price suppression or rapid buying and selling to create market turbulence, to longer-term strategies that involve the accumulation or distribution of assets. However, it's crucial to recognize that not all actions of smart money are indicative of manipulation; many are driven by astute, research-driven decisions.

In truth, smart money's actions can be a double-edged sword for market participants. On one hand, they possess the capability to offer valuable insights into potential market trends. Their decisions often stem from exhaustive research, sophisticated models, and expert analysis. As a result, their moves can serve as leading indicators, providing cues that guide other investors in their own decision-making processes.

However, the motivations behind smart money's actions may not always align with the broader market's interests. They frequently prioritize their own objectives, which may involve achieving short-term profits, hedging against risks, or strategically positioning themselves in anticipation of future developments. Consequently, their interests can diverge from those of retail investors and other market participants seeking stability and consistent returns.

The key to discerning whether smart money's activities constitute market manipulation or genuine insight lies in a nuanced analysis of their actions, intentions, and their broader impact. Regulatory bodies play a crucial role in monitoring and enforcing market integrity, ensuring that manipulative practices are identified and addressed. Transparency and accountability are essential in maintaining trust within financial markets, as they provide a framework for distinguishing between ethical trading and illicit activities.

In the ever-evolving landscape of finance, the question of smart money's true intentions remains a dynamic and complex one. While their influence cannot be denied, it is imperative that market participants and regulatory authorities remain vigilant, fostering an environment where true market insight can thrive while manipulation is rooted out and appropriately addressed.

READING THE FOOTPRINTS: UNRAVELING THE STRATEGIES OF SMART MONEY

For traders and market enthusiasts, uncovering the elusive footprints left by smart money is akin to solving a complex puzzle. These discerning investors often employ an array of indicators and techniques to gain insights into the strategies being employed by institutional giants, hedge funds, and seasoned professional traders. This practice serves as a means to tap into the wisdom of these market mavens and anticipate potential market shifts.

Volume patterns, a fundamental starting point for many, offer a crucial window into the market's dynamics. By analyzing trading volume, traders can identify anomalies that may hint at smart money's involvement. Sudden surges in volume, particularly in conjunction with price movements, can be a telltale sign of institutional activity. These spikes often precede significant market developments, acting as a signal that attracts the attention of astute traders.

Another avenue to deciphering smart money's intentions is by tracking large institutional orders. This involves monitoring the execution of sizable trades that go beyond the typical retail investor's capacity. Institutional players often execute trades in blocks, and detecting these substantial transactions can provide insights into their sentiment and potential market positioning. Such large orders can reveal a commitment to a particular trade, offering valuable cues for those who observe them closely.

Options activity is yet another intriguing realm where traders seek clues about smart money's strategies. By monitoring options contracts and their movements, one can glean information about potential market shifts. Unusual options volume, particularly around key strike prices or expiry dates, can be indicative of significant market anticipation or hedging strategies. This type of information can serve as a guide to traders aiming to align their positions with the smart money.

Price action around critical support and resistance levels is a treasure trove of information for market enthusiasts. These levels are key thresholds where supply and demand dynamics often collide. Smart money's actions, such as accumulation or distribution of assets, can leave distinctive imprints on price charts. Observing how price behaves at these junctures can provide insights into whether smart money is entering or exiting positions, and the direction they may be leaning towards.

In sum, these techniques for interpreting the footprints of smart money allow traders to gain valuable hints about potential market directions. While not foolproof, they serve as a lens through which traders can make more informed decisions and position themselves strategically in the market. This ongoing quest to decode the strategies of smart money exemplifies the dynamic and ever-evolving nature of financial markets, where knowledge and insight are prized commodities.

Retail vs. Smart Money: The Intricate Game of Chess in the Financial Arena

The world of financial markets resembles an intricate game of chess, where retail traders and smart money players are the key adversaries in an ongoing strategic battle. This battle unfolds daily, with each side carefully plotting their moves to gain an edge in the ever-shifting landscape of investments. Understanding the strategies and actions of smart money is an invaluable skill for retail traders, akin to learning the tactics of a seasoned opponent in a game of chess. It can provide them with the insight and knowledge needed to navigate the markets effectively.

Smart money, comprising institutional investors, hedge funds, and experienced professional traders, brings a formidable arsenal to this strategic contest. Their deep pockets, extensive resources, and access to advanced research and technology afford them an advantage. They operate on a grand scale, often making substantial investments that ripple through the market, and their positions may be tailored for the long term. In this grand chess game, smart money can be seen as the masters of opening and mid-game strategies, positioning themselves with a focus on the long-term outlook.

On the other side of the board, retail traders, with their individual accounts and often limited resources, play a different game. Their decisions are more agile, influenced by a shorter-term perspective, and they must constantly adapt to changing market conditions. It's essential for them to be keen observers, learning from the moves and counter-moves of smart money and other market participants.

The ability to comprehend smart money's maneuvers offers retail traders a strategic advantage. By tracking large orders, detecting unusual volume patterns, and monitoring options activity, they can anticipate potential market shifts and adjust their positions accordingly. This knowledge empowers them to act more decisively and make informed decisions, enhancing their chances of success in the market.

However, it's crucial to acknowledge that smart money and retail traders play by different rules. Smart money's decisions, often rooted in comprehensive research and longer-term considerations, may not align with the retail trader's short-term goals. Retail traders must be mindful of these disparities and recognize that while they can draw inspiration from smart money's strategies, they need to adapt them to their own circumstances.

In conclusion, the ongoing battle between retail traders and smart money resembles a high-stakes chess match, with each side employing its unique set of skills and resources. Understanding the strategies and motivations of smart money can be a valuable asset for retail traders, helping them make informed decisions in a complex and dynamic financial landscape. By recognizing the differences in scale and timeline between the two sides, retail traders can navigate this intricate game of chess more effectively, capitalizing on the insights gleaned from their formidable opponents.

BALANCING RETAIL STRATEGIES: UNLOCKING POTENTIAL AMIDST THE SMART MONEY INFLUENCE

In a financial landscape where smart money casts a significant shadow, it's paramount to understand that not all retail traders are relegated to the role of passive observers. While the institutional behemoths and seasoned professionals undoubtedly wield considerable influence, retail traders possess the capacity to adapt and even thrive by embracing elements of smart money concepts within their own strategies. In this intricate dance between David and Goliath, retail traders have the opportunity to level the playing field and enhance their decision-making prowess.

Adapting to the presence of smart money begins with a comprehensive analysis of market data. Retail traders can no longer afford to rely solely on gut instincts or surface-level information. They must delve into the depths of market research, employing tools and techniques that help them uncover valuable insights. By harnessing technical and fundamental analysis, they can develop a holistic understanding of the market's dynamics, trends, and potential opportunities. Additionally, staying abreast of macroeconomic events and global financial news is vital, as these factors often drive smart money's decisions.

One of the key strategies for retail traders is to remain informed about institutional actions. Observing the footprints left by smart money, such as tracking large institutional orders and monitoring options activity, allows retail traders to anticipate potential market shifts. The ability to read between the lines of market activity and discern the motivations behind large-scale transactions is a skill that can provide a substantial advantage.

This knowledge empowers retail traders to position themselves strategically and make informed decisions that align with their own objectives.

Moreover, retail traders can also benefit from diversifying their trading strategies. While smart money often deploys a wide array of tactics, retail traders can expand their toolkit by incorporating techniques such as day trading, swing trading, or long-term investing, depending on their risk tolerance and goals. This flexibility enables them to adapt to various market conditions and seize opportunities that align with their chosen trading horizon.

In conclusion, while the influence of smart money remains a formidable force, it's important to recognize that retail traders have the potential to navigate this complex landscape successfully. By incorporating smart money concepts into their strategies, including thorough market analysis, staying informed about institutional actions, and developing a nuanced understanding of market dynamics, retail traders can enhance their decision-making abilities. This adaptability empowers them to effectively coexist with smart money, leveraging their own strengths and insights to carve a path to success in the ever-evolving world of financial markets.

THE QUEST FOR INSIGHT: NAVIGATING THE COMPLEXITIES OF FINANCIAL MARKETS THROUGH SMART MONEY CONCEPTS

The world of financial markets is a dynamic and intricate realm, where countless factors influence asset prices, and market sentiment can shift in an instant. Amidst this complexity, the concept of smart money serves as a beacon, shedding light on the hidden currents that shape these markets. By gaining a deeper understanding of the mindset and strategies employed by institutional players, traders embark on a quest for insight that can provide them with a unique vantage point.

Smart money isn't a monolithic entity; it encompasses a diverse range of market participants, from large institutional investors and hedge funds to seasoned professional traders. Each of these players brings a distinctive set of skills, resources, and strategies to the table. As a result, peering into the world of smart money unveils a rich tapestry of market behaviors and tactics.

What makes smart money concepts so compelling is their potential to reveal the underlying motivations behind significant market movements. By scrutinizing the actions of institutional players, traders can discern the factors influencing their investment decisions. This can include comprehensive market research, advanced technical and fundamental analysis, and a keen awareness of macroeconomic trends. Additionally, it often involves the ability to identify inflection points in the market, recognizing moments of over-exuberance or undue pessimism.

However, it's crucial to acknowledge that smart money is

not infallible, and its insights do not guarantee success. Market conditions are subject to a multitude of variables, and unpredictability is an inherent characteristic of financial markets. Despite this, integrating smart money insights into one's trading strategies can significantly elevate a trader's ability to navigate these complexities.

The knowledge acquired through the study of smart money can act as a guiding compass, helping traders make more informed decisions. While it may not eliminate all the risks and uncertainties that come with trading, it does offer a more robust framework for evaluating potential investment opportunities and managing risk. This heightened level of awareness empowers traders to adapt to evolving market conditions, seize opportunities, and mitigate threats more effectively.

In conclusion, the quest for insight through smart money concepts represents a valuable endeavor for traders in the ever-changing financial landscape. It is not a panacea, but rather a powerful tool that equips traders with the knowledge and perspective necessary to thrive amidst the complexities of financial markets. By embracing these insights, traders embark on a continuous journey of learning and adaptation, striving for a competitive edge in their pursuit of success.

1. MARKET STRUCTURE

Understanding the Dynamics of an Uptrend

Market structure is a critical concept in the world of finance that provides a framework for analyzing and interpreting the dynamics of various market conditions and trends. One essential aspect of market structure is the identification and comprehension of different market trends, with one of the most commonly observed being the uptrend.

An uptrend, in the context of market structure, is a prevailing pattern in which the prices of assets, such as stocks, commodities, or currencies, are moving generally upward over a specific time period. This trend signifies a period of optimism and positive sentiment among market participants, often characterized by increased demand for these assets. Understanding the components and implications of an uptrend is of paramount importance for investors, traders, and analysts as it can offer valuable insights for decision-making and strategy development.

Key Characteristics of an Uptrend:
1. **Higher Highs and Higher Lows:** The defining feature of an uptrend is a sequence of higher highs and higher lows. This means that as time progresses, the price of the asset reaches higher peaks (highs) and does not retreat to previous low points (lows) by the same magnitude. This pattern reflects a gradual, sustained increase in asset prices.

2. **Bullish Momentum:** Uptrends are typically associated with bullish momentum, where buyers outnumber sellers in the market. This can be driven by positive news, strong economic indicators, or favorable sentiment about a particular asset or market.

3. **Support Levels:** During an uptrend, support levels often emerge, acting as price floors where the asset's value tends to find buying interest. These support levels indicate the point at which buyers are willing to step in and prevent the price from declining significantly.

4. **Moving Averages:** Analysts often use moving averages, such as the simple moving average (SMA) or the exponential moving average (EMA), to confirm and track uptrends. When the price remains consistently above the moving average, it reinforces the notion of an ongoing uptrend.

5. **Volume:** An uptrend is typically accompanied by increasing trading volume. Higher trading volumes suggest strong market participation and support the credibility of the uptrend.

Implications and Considerations: Understanding an uptrend has several practical implications for market participants:

1. **Investment Opportunities:** For long-term investors, recognizing an uptrend can signal potential investment opportunities. Buying and holding assets during an uptrend may yield significant returns as prices appreciate.

2. **Trading Strategies:** Traders often employ various strategies to capitalize on uptrends, such as trend following, swing trading, or momentum trading. These approaches involve buying assets with the expectation that their value will continue to rise.

3. **Risk Management**: It's essential to manage risk even in an uptrend. Recognizing potential reversals and implementing stop-loss orders can help protect gains and limit losses.

4. **Diversification**: Diversifying a portfolio across different asset classes can mitigate the risks associated with a single uptrend, as not all assets will move in the same direction simultaneously.

5. **Economic and Fundamental Analysis**: Understanding the underlying economic factors and fundamentals driving an uptrend is crucial. Economic indicators, corporate earnings reports, and geopolitical events can impact the sustainability of the trend.

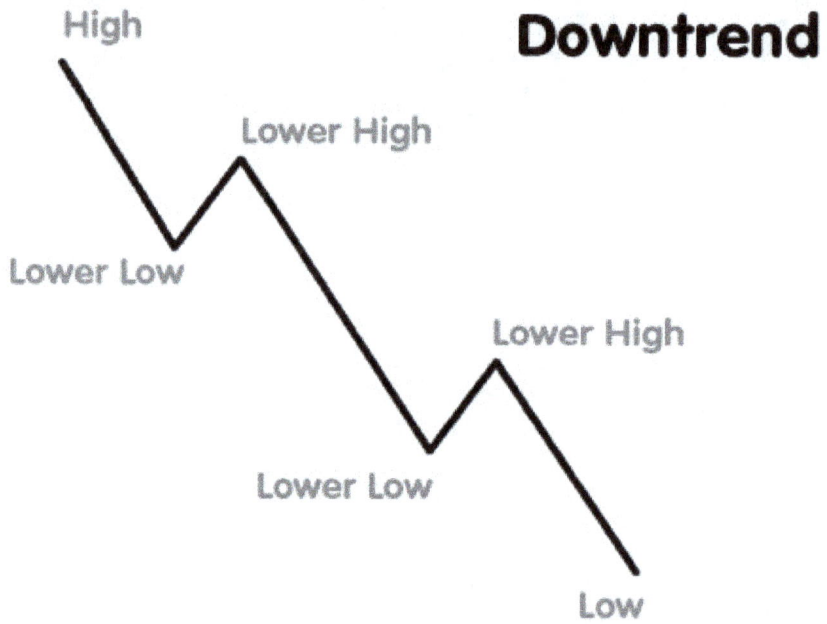

Downtrend

MARKET STRUCTURE: THE DEPTHS OF A DOWNTREND

Market structure, a fundamental concept in the field of finance, serves as a guiding framework for understanding the intricate patterns and trends that shape financial markets. Among the myriad market conditions, one of the most significant and often impactful is the downtrend. A downtrend, as a component of market structure, represents a period of sustained price declines for assets like stocks, commodities, or currencies over a specific timeframe. Recognizing the features and implications of a downtrend is paramount for market participants, enabling them to make informed decisions and implement sound risk management strategies.

Key Characteristics of a Downtrend:

1. **Lower Highs and Lower Lows**: The defining feature of a downtrend is a sequence of lower highs and lower lows. This means that over time, the asset's price forms progressively lower peaks (highs) and fails to recover to previous high points (lows). This recurring pattern reflects a continuous decline in the asset's value.

2. **Bearish Momentum**: Downtrends are typically associated with bearish momentum, where sellers outnumber buyers in the market. This negative sentiment is often driven by unfavorable news, deteriorating economic indicators, or pessimism regarding specific assets or market conditions.

3. **Resistance Levels**: Within a downtrend, resistance levels tend to emerge, acting as price ceilings where the asset's value encounters selling pressure. These resistance levels

denote the points at which sellers intervene to curtail price increases.

4. **Moving Averages**: Analysts often employ moving averages, such as the simple moving average (SMA) or the exponential moving average (EMA), to confirm and track downtrends. When the asset's price consistently remains below the moving average, it reinforces the notion of an ongoing downtrend.

5. **Volume**: Downtrends are typically accompanied by heightened trading volume. Increased trading volumes indicate robust market participation, underscoring the credibility of the downtrend.

Implications and Considerations:

Understanding the intricacies of a downtrend has several critical implications for market participants:

1. **Short-Selling Opportunities**: For traders, downtrends often offer opportunities for short selling, a strategy in which assets are sold with the anticipation of buying them back at lower prices. This approach allows traders to profit from declining prices.

2. **Risk Management**: Downtrends pose risks to investors and traders. Implementing risk management strategies, such as stop-loss orders, is essential to safeguard capital and limit potential losses should the market reverse.

3. **Contrarian Strategies**: Some investors may adopt contrarian strategies within a downtrend, seeking assets that may have been oversold and could potentially rebound. While this approach carries higher risk, it can yield substantial rewards.

4. **Economic and Fundamental Analysis**: Understanding the underlying economic factors and fundamentals that drive a downtrend is crucial. Economic indicators, corporate earnings reports, and geopolitical events can significantly impact the sustainability of the downtrend.

5. **Diversification**: Diversifying a portfolio across various asset classes can help mitigate the risks associated with a single downtrend. Diversification ensures that not all assets move in the same direction, providing stability to the overall portfolio.

; CONSOLIDATION

Market Structure: The Intricate Dynamics of Consolidation

In the realm of finance, market structure serves as the foundational framework for comprehending the various patterns and trends that define the behavior of financial markets. One of the distinctive phases in market structure is consolidation, a condition that often characterizes a period of relative price stability and market indecision. Understanding the intricacies and implications of consolidation is of paramount importance for investors, traders, and analysts, as it offers valuable insights into market sentiment and can inform strategic decision-making and risk management.

Key Characteristics of Consolidation:

1. **Sideways Price Movement**: The most recognizable feature of consolidation is a prolonged period of sideways or horizontal price movement. During this phase, asset prices neither exhibit a clear upward nor downward trend, and they generally trade within a defined price range. This lateral movement is marked by a series of higher lows and lower highs, resulting in a price channel or range.

2. **Decreased Volatility**: Consolidation is often accompanied by reduced price volatility. This implies that the asset's price fluctuations become more limited, reflecting a sense of equilibrium in the market. Traders may notice that price swings are less dramatic during this phase.

3. **Market Indecision**: Consolidation is a manifestation of

market indecision. Investors and traders are typically hesitant or uncertain about the asset's future direction. This uncertainty is often driven by external factors, such as pending economic reports, political events, or earnings announcements, that create a wait-and-see attitude among market participants.

4. **Support and Resistance Levels**: Within a consolidation pattern, distinct support and resistance levels emerge. Support represents a price level at which buying interest increases, preventing the price from declining further, while resistance is a price level where selling pressure increases, preventing the price from rising. These levels mark the upper and lower boundaries of the price range.

5. **Declining Volume**: In many cases, trading volume tends to decrease during consolidation. As market participants await a catalyst for price movement, trading activity can dwindle, indicating a sense of uncertainty among traders and investors.

Implications and Considerations:

Understanding consolidation in the context of market structure has several notable implications for market participants:

1. **Trend Reversal or Continuation**: Consolidation can serve as a transitional phase in which market participants await a clear signal. It can lead to either a trend continuation, where the asset's previous direction resumes, or a trend reversal, where the asset takes on a new trajectory. Traders must remain vigilant for the eventual breakout from consolidation, as it can provide significant trading opportunities.

2. **Risk Management**: For traders, consolidation can pose challenges, as it may result in false breakouts or whipsaw movements. Implementing robust risk management techniques, such as setting stop-loss orders or trailing

stops, is crucial to mitigate potential losses.

3. **Patience and Timing**: In a consolidation phase, patience is a virtue. Traders may need to wait for a clear breakout from the range before taking action. Timing the market and making informed decisions when the consolidation pattern resolves is vital.

4. **Range-Bound Strategies**: Traders may employ range-bound strategies during consolidation, buying at support levels and selling at resistance levels. This approach seeks to profit from the predictable price movements within the consolidation range.

5. **Fundamental Analysis**: To anticipate the direction of an asset following consolidation, investors and traders should consider the fundamental factors that may act as catalysts. Events such as economic data releases, corporate earnings reports, or geopolitical developments can influence the breakout direction.

CONSOLIDATION

Consolidation is a technical analysis term used to describe a stock's price movement within a given support and resistance range for a period of time.

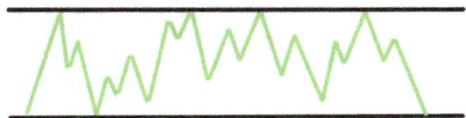

2. EXPANSION AND

RETRACEMENT

EXPANSION

Occurs when there is an impulsive movement towards a direction.

RETRACEMENT

Is the correction movement after an impulsive move.

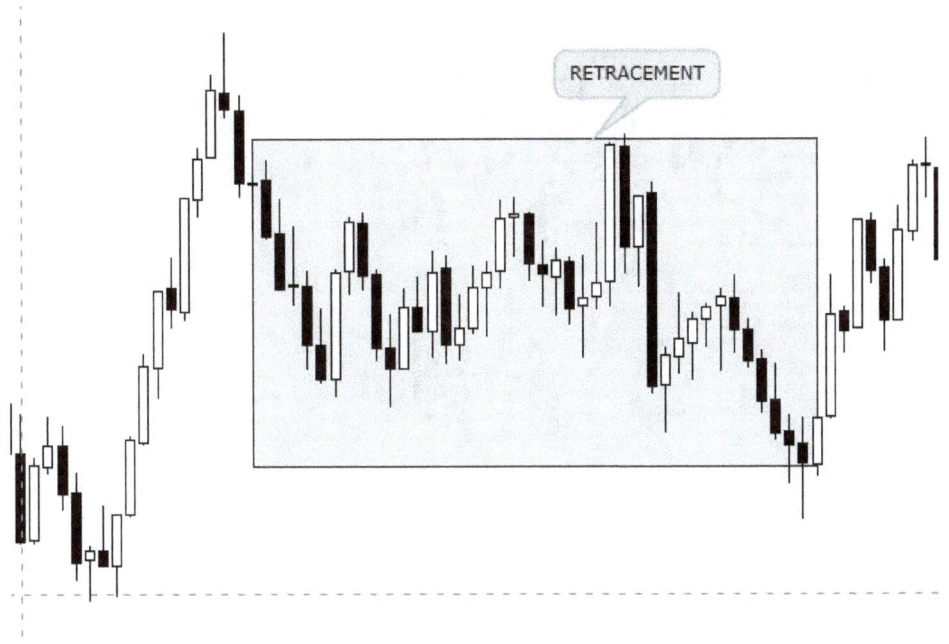

3. ORDER BLOCKS (OB)

The market returns to those candles and they are never violated.

TYPES OF ORDER BLOCKS

: Bullish order block

: Bearish order block

BULLISH ORDER BLOCK

: Is the last candle before the bullish movement, which breaks the market structure higher.

: Represents a high possibility of holding the price when it returns to it.

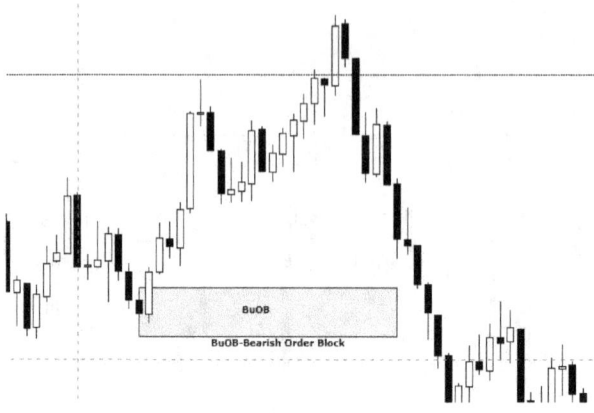

BEARISH ORDER BLOCK

; Is the last bullish candle before the bearish movement that breaks the market structure lower.

: Represents a high possibility of holding the price, when the price returns to it.

<u>CHARACTERISTICS OF TRADABLE ORDER BLOCKS</u>

1.   OB SHOULD BE AT/NEAR SUPPORT/RESISTANCE

2. OB SHOULD BE AT/NEAR FLIP ZONE (Good for reversal entries)

3. OB MUST BREAK THE MARKET STRUCTURE [BMS]

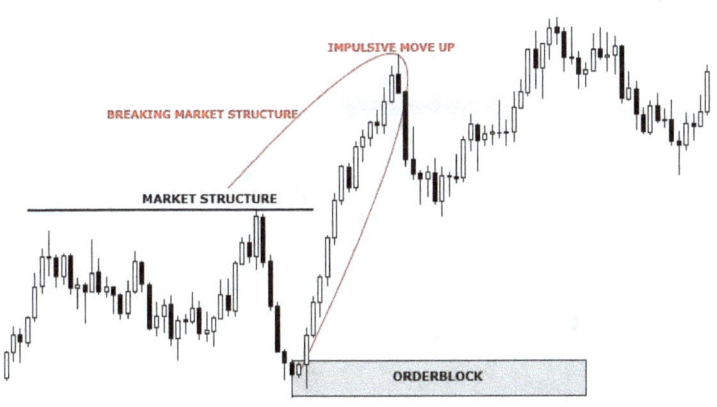

4. IMBALANCE

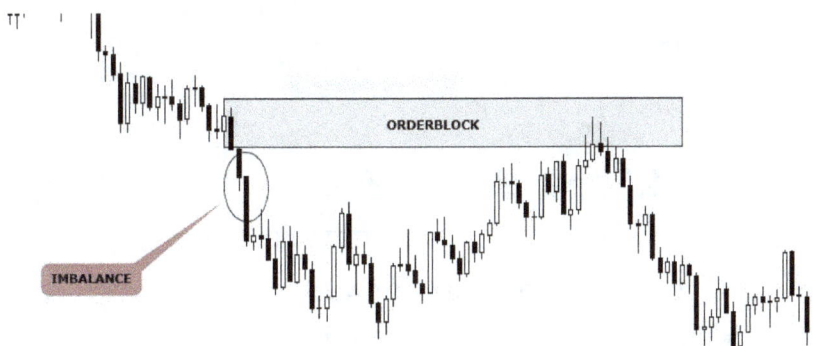

5.   BULLISH OB ABOVE EQH.

6.   BEARISH OB BELOW EQL.

<u>HOW TO TRADE ORDERBLOCKS</u>

1. STOP HUNT, BREAK OF MARKET STRUCTURE AND RETURN TO ORDER BLOCK (SH, BMS AND RTO)

1. Banks take liquidity (SH)

*Stop Hunt (SH): Hunting for stop losses of retail traders.

2. There is BMS confirming SH

*BMS is caused by impulsive move from the order block.

3. Price return to OB

*The price return to an order block in a correction form (retracement)

Using BuOB

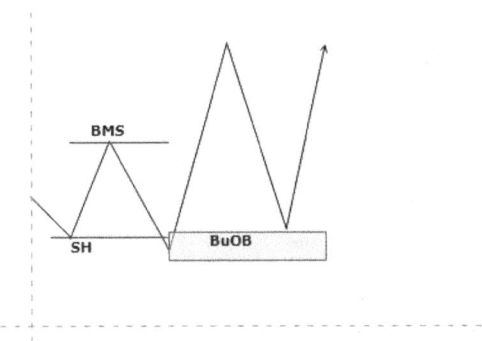

Example 1

*After marking Stop Hunt, Break of Market Structure and

Order Block ,We wait for the market to return to our order block so that we enter our buy signal.

*Normally our TP1 is the first high.

Example 2

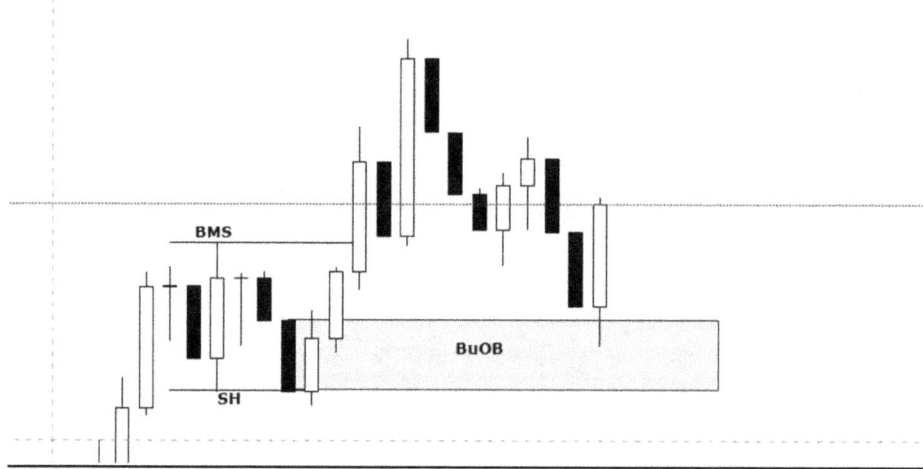

Same as setup 1, firstly,

* Identify the SH and OB

*Then break of market structure

*Wait for RTO, So that we can place our orders

2. SHIFT OF MARKET STRUCTURE +BREAK OF MARET STRUCTURE + RETURN TO ORDER BLOCK

(SMS +BMS+RTO)

1. Price fails to break a higher high or higher low.

2. There is break of market structure (BMS), Confirming SMS

3. The price returns to OB

USING BEOB

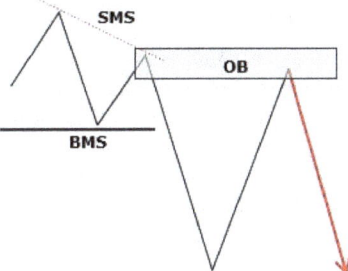

Example 1

Example 2

Using BuOB

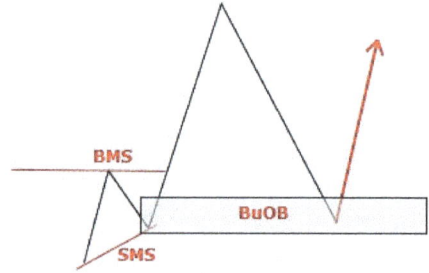

Example 1

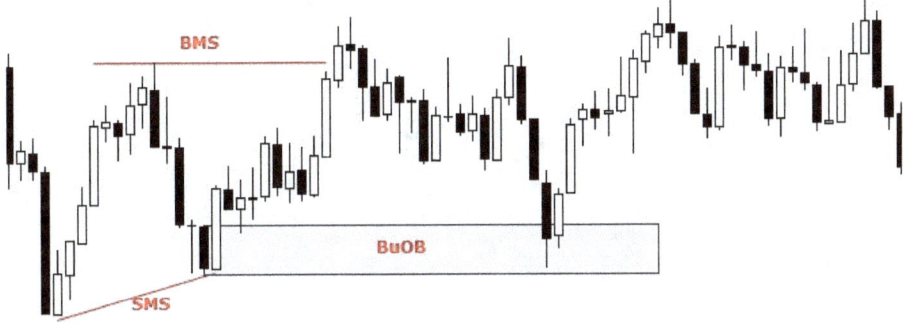

Example 2

3.BREAKER BLOCKS

We have two types of breaker blocks.

*Bullish breaker block

*Bearish breaker block

HOW TO TRADE BEARISH BREAKER BLOCK AND BULLISH BREAKER BLOCK

BEARISH BREAKER BLOCK

*A bearish breaker block occurs when price creates a lower low ,collecting liquidity pools by taking out the previous low then pull up and collect buy side liquidity on the nearest high then price will come back later to retest the previous violated high and continue to go down.

This happens to close all liquidity voids created, and our main goal is to wait for a pullback to the previous high and once we see a good rejection we make our buy entries.

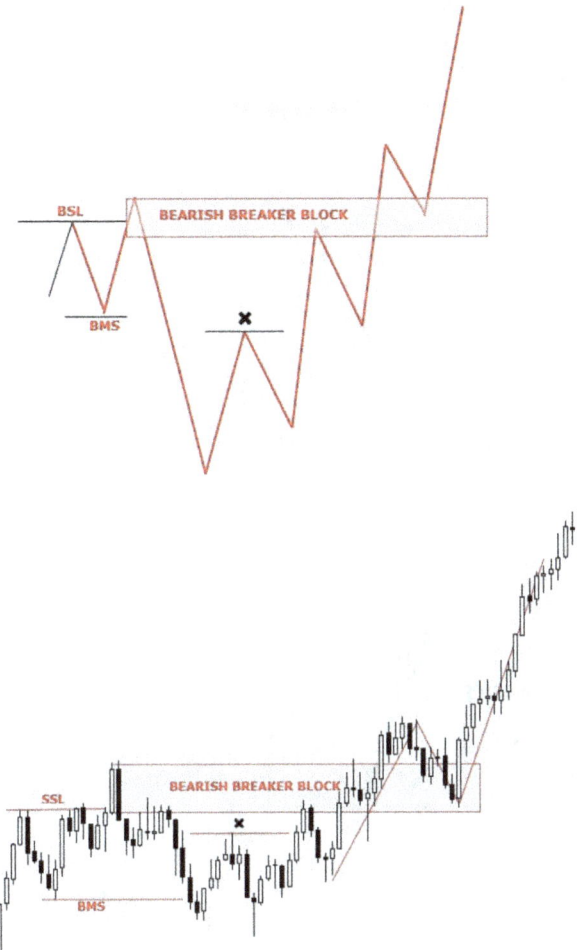

BULLISH BREAKER BLOCK

A bullish breaker block occurs, When price creates a higher high , collecting all the resting liquidity pools on previous highs forming a higher high ,then price will drop and collect sell side liquidity on previous lows and forms a lower low ,after that price will retrace up to the previous violated low and retest then continue to drop ,that's where we will take advantage of price and sell short on the previously violated low.

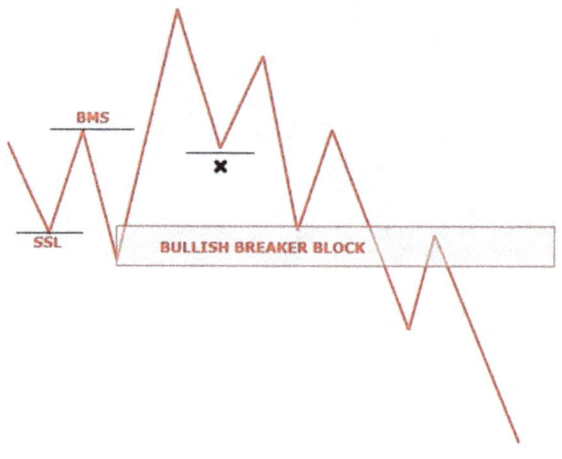

BMS

SSL

bullish breaker block

4. ACCUMULATION, MANIPULATION AND DISTRIBUTION

(AMD)

HOW TO TRADE AMD

1. Accumulation: The price will be ranging

2. Manipulation: The price will break the range direction to trap traders (Because of liquidity)

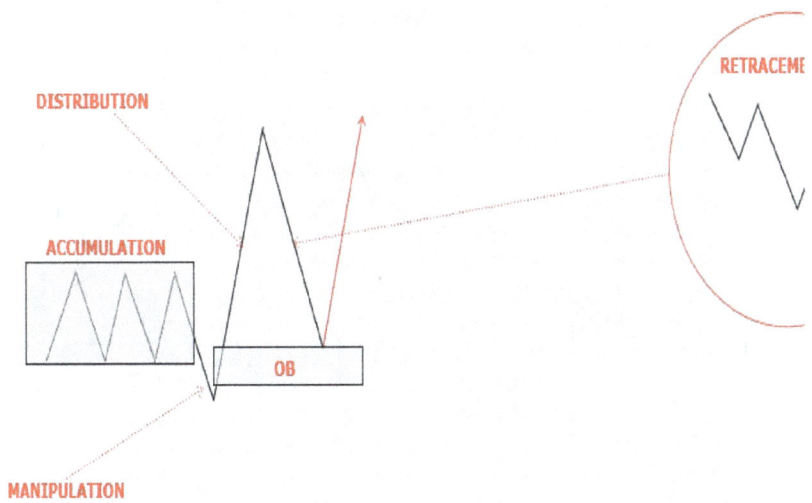

3. Distribution: The price will go against the manipulation movement, and here look to go long/short by using (SH+BMS +RTO/SMS+BMS+RTO)

EXAMPLE 1

Example 2

5. LIQUIDITY

The liquidity is defined by the stop losses, where the stop losses exist is where the liquidity exist.

Smart money need to activate the stop losses of existing orders in the market so they can place their positions in the market.

The banks manipulate the price because of liquidity.

TYPES OF LIQUIDITY

*Buy side liquidity (BSL)

*Sell side liquidity (SSL)

WHAT FORMS LIQUIDITY

1. Equal highs

2. Equal lows

4. Flip zones

5. Inducements

6. Trendline liquidity

*BSL:Stop losses of sell orders ,after the bsl is taken ,the market will reverse to the downside ,because the banks use the BSL to place sell orders in the market.

*SSL: Stop losses of the buy orders, after the ssl is taken, the market will reverse to the upside because banks use the SSL to place orders in the market.

STOP HUNT: Manipulation for liquidity

SH is a movement used to neutralize liquidity (stop losses).Is a false breakout above or below the zone where there is liquidity.

DEMONSTRATION

1. Buy side liquidity

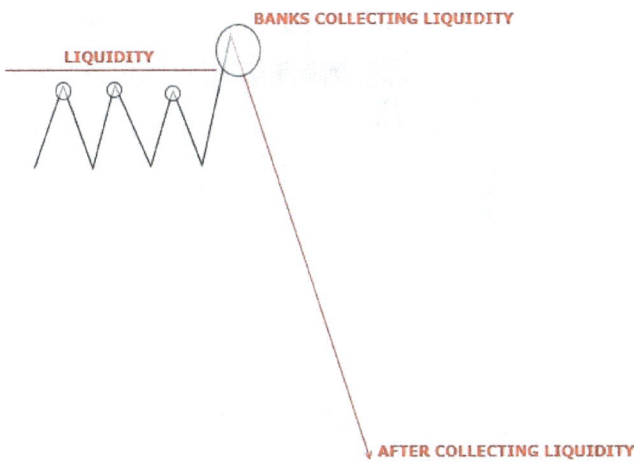

Buy side liquidity created by resistance zone.
Banks manipulate the price to collect BSL, because banks use bsl to place sell orders.

EXAMPLE 1

Example 2

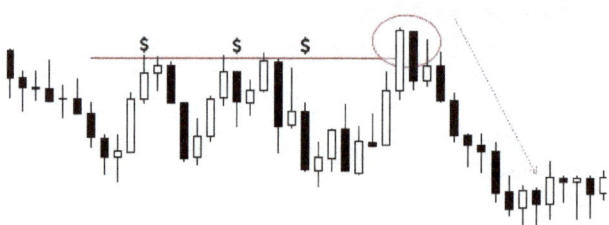

2. Sell side liquidity

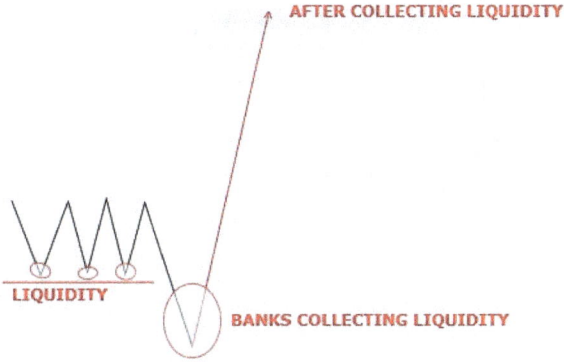

Sell side liquidity is created by support level.

Banks manipulate the price to collect **SSL** because banks use **SSL** to place buy orders.

Example 1

Example 2

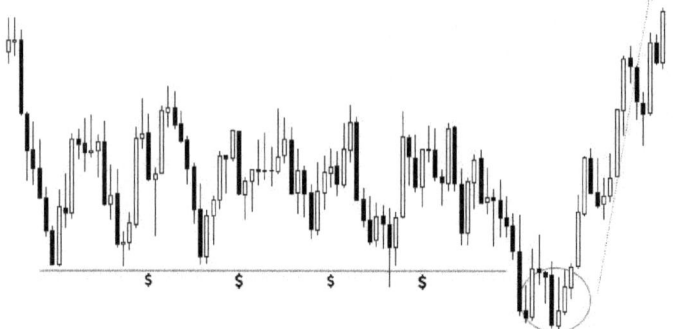

RS FLIP ZONES RESISTANCE TURNING TO SUPPORT

RS FLIP (resistance turning into support)

Trading support-turned-resistance flip zones is a common strategy used by traders to identify potential reversal points in the market.

These zones occur when a level that was previously acting as support (where price stopped declining) becomes a barrier to further price movement as resistance (where price struggles to move above).

Here is a systematic guide on how to trade these flip zones:

1. **Identify Key Support Levels:** Start by identifying significant support levels on the price chart. These are areas where price has previously halted its decline and reversed direction.

2. **Monitor Price Behavior:** Once a support level is identified, observe how price behaves around that level. If price approaches the support level and starts to bounce, it indicates that the support level is holding. This could potentially be a flip zone in the making.

3. **Wait for Confirmation:** A key principle of trading flip zones is waiting for confirmation that the support has indeed turned into resistance. To do this, watch for price to approach the former support level and then stall or reverse around that area.

4. **Look for Price Rejection:** Look for signs of price rejection as it nears the former support level. This could be in the form of candlestick patterns (e.g., bearish engulfing, shooting star) or a series of lower highs forming around the area.

5. **Lower Timeframe Analysis:** Zoom in to lower timeframes (e.g., 1-hour, 15-minute) to get a more detailed view of price action around the potential flip zone. Look for signs of consolidation, indecision, or bearish price movements around the area.

6. **Entry Strategy:** Once you have confirmation of a potential flip zone, consider entering a trade. A common approach is to place a short (sell) order slightly below the confirmed resistance level. This can act as a buffer in case price tests the level before reversing.

7. **Set Stop-Loss and Take-Profit:** Place a stop-loss order just above the confirmed resistance level. This helps protect your trade in case the price breaks through the flip zone. Set a take-profit order at a reasonable target level, considering the potential for a price reversal.

8. **Risk Management:** Determine your position size based on your risk tolerance and the distance between your entry point and stop-loss level. Ensure that you are not risking more than a predetermined percentage of your trading capital on the trade.

9. **Monitor Price Action:** As the trade progresses, closely monitor price action and market developments. If price approaches your take-profit level and shows signs of stalling, consider manually closing the trade to secure profits.

10. **Adapt to Market Conditions:** Keep in mind that not all flip zones will result in successful trades. Be prepared to adapt and cut losses if the market does not behave as expected. Flexibility is key in trading.

11. **Use Additional Confirmation Tools:** To strengthen your analysis, consider using other technical indicators or tools, such as trend lines, moving averages, or volume analysis that align with your assessment of the flip zone.

Liquidity exists below these zones

Example

How to trade RS flip?

After identifying the RS flip zone, use an order block below the zone as your entry point.

SR FLIP ZONES

SR FLIP (support turning into resistance) Liquidity also exists above these zones.

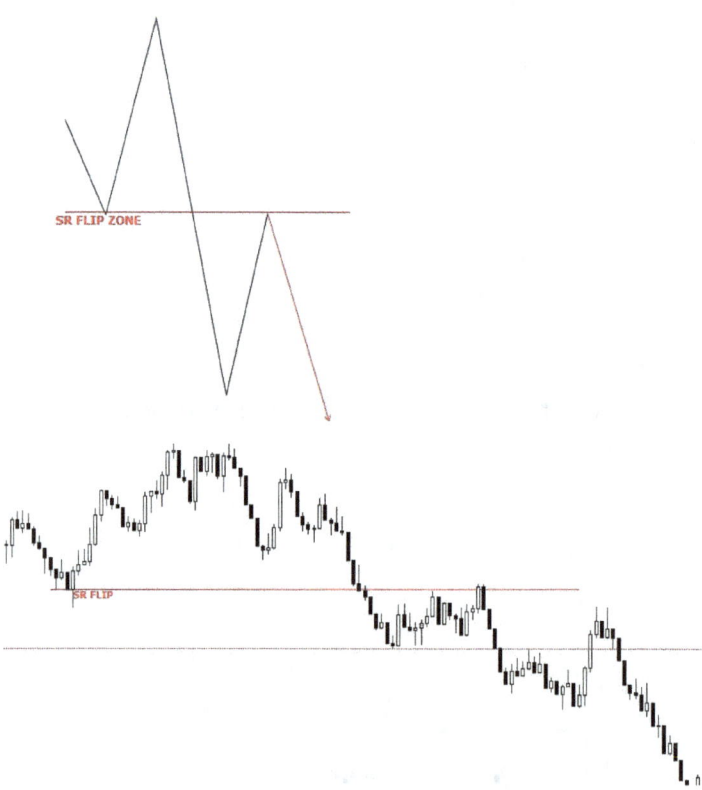

How to trade SR flip?

After identifying the SR flip zone,use an order block below the zone as your entry point.

INDUCEMENT

Accumulation of retailers in seek of liquidity.

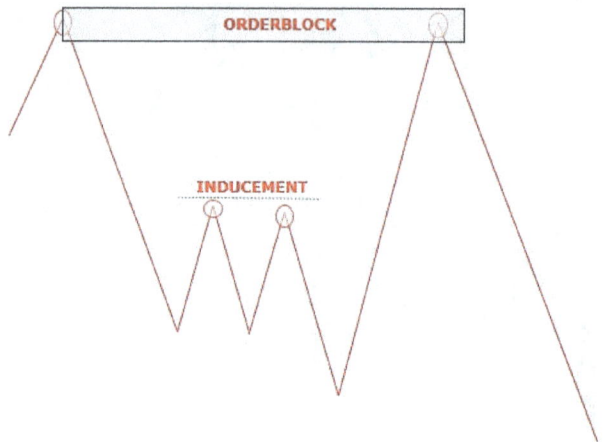

Example 1

Example 2

IMBALANCES

Imbalances occurs when either buyers or sellers take control over a particular piece of price action ,which will essentially leave gaps in the market that price will come back to in the future to re balance the price.

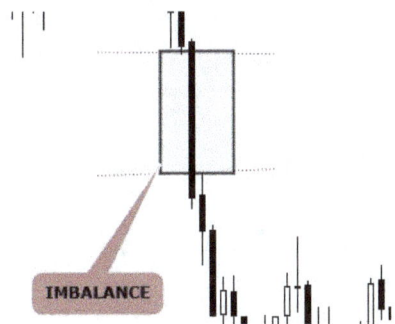

HOW TO TRADE AN IMBALANCE

Example 2

6. ADDING CONFLUENCE

Confluence is very important because it increases the chances of winning trades, a trader needs to have at least two factors of confluence to open a trade.

When the confluence exists, the trader becomes more confident on his setups.

Factors of confluence can be,

*Combining setups

*Refine high time frames key levels in lower time frames for entries

* In some cases you can use trend lines to increase confluence.

Example 1

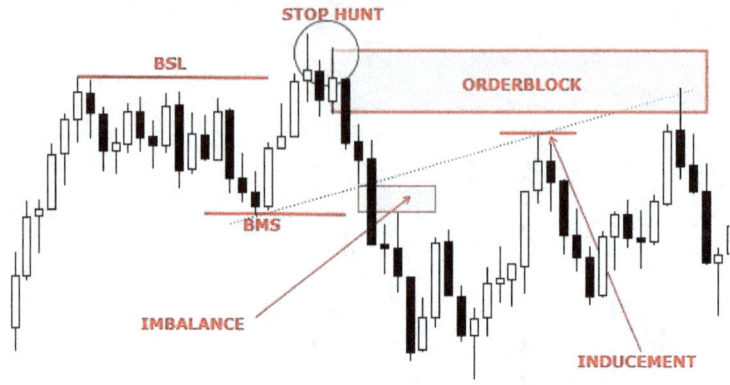

Example 2

ENTRIES

Understanding how Smart Money & Retail Traders participate in the market will help you to also understand how to trade with Smart Money.

Types of entries

*Aggressive entries

*Confirmation entries

AGGRESSIVE ENTRIES

This is a risk entry that does not require any confirmation.

Identify an order block and wait for price (with pending order) to come back to it.

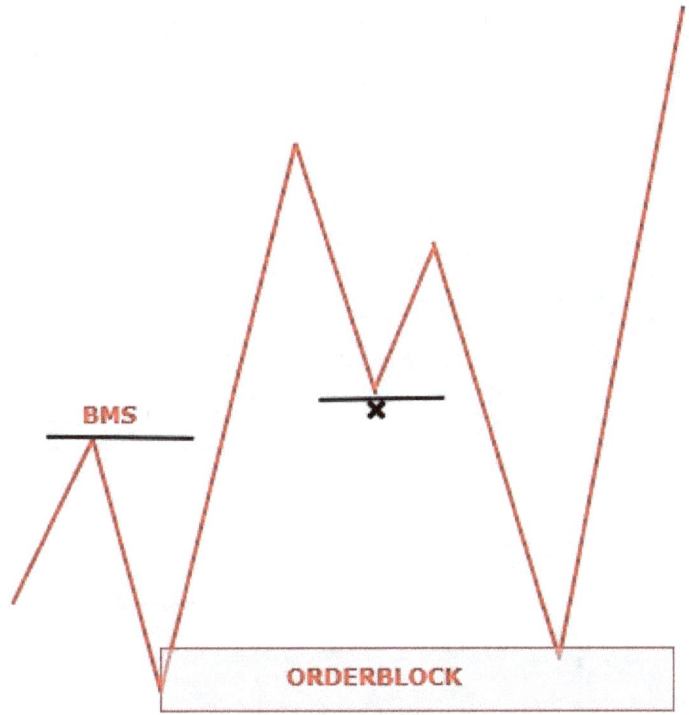

Example

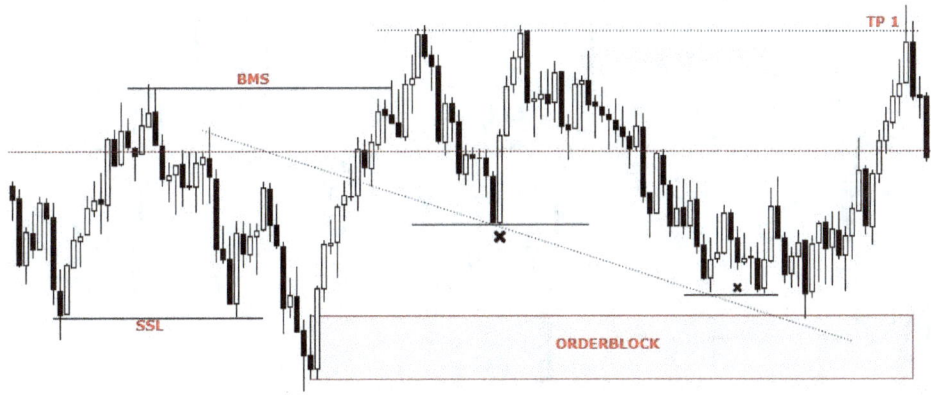

2. CONFIRMATION ENTRY

This is conservative entry that require confirmation, especially from HTF (Must do Top-Down Analysis).

Identify POI on HTF & refine it to LTF.

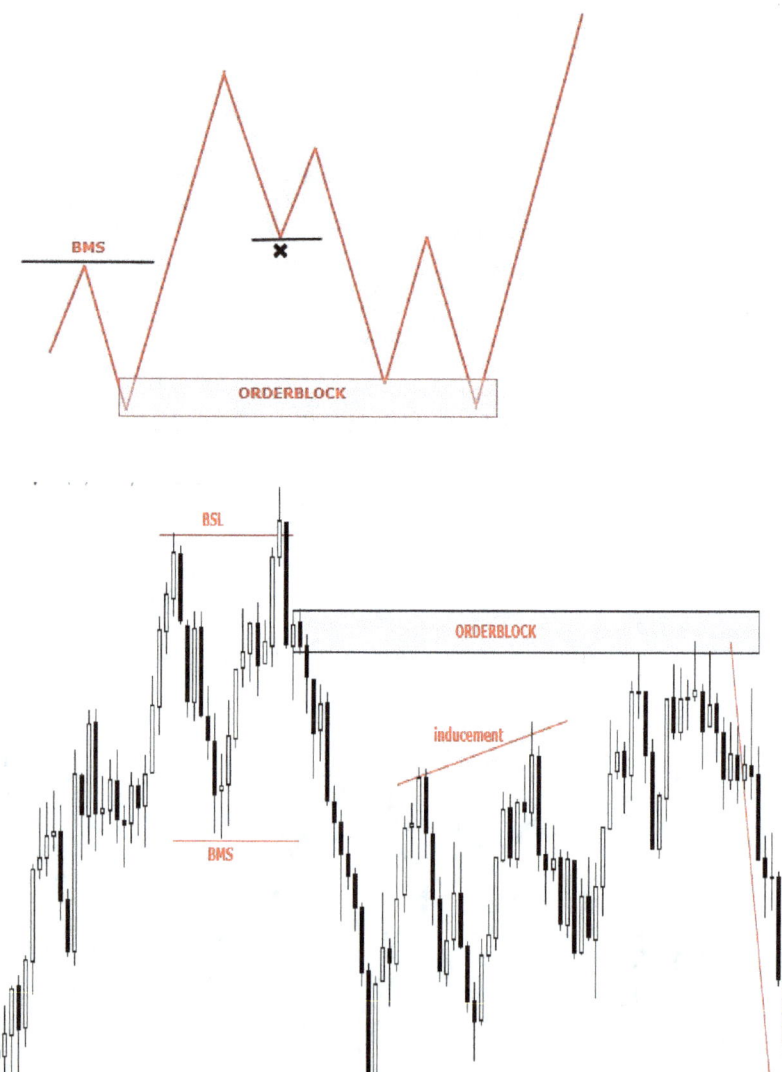

Example

REMEMBER

*Having a great analysis does not make you a great trader, the execution part is more important because that were you deal with emotions.

* So you being a trader consist of being executing trades.

* Lastly consistency requires proper risk management.

DEALING WITH EMOTIONS
WHILE TRADING

- **Self-Awareness**: Recognize and acknowledge your emotions. Understand how fear, greed, excitement, and frustration can impact your decision-making.

- **Education**: Learn about trading strategies, market dynamics, and risk management. Knowledge empowers you to make informed decisions and reduces emotional reactions.

- **Trading Plan**: Create a detailed trading plan that includes entry and exit criteria, risk management rules, and contingencies for different scenarios. Following a plan reduces emotional trading.

- **Risk Management**: Determine how much of your capital you're willing to risk on each trade. Set stop-loss orders to limit potential losses and protect your capital.

- **Position Sizing**: Calculate your position size based on your risk tolerance and stop-loss level. Avoid risking too much of your capital on a single trade.

- **Practice Patience**: Wait for valid trade setups that align with your strategy. Avoid jumping into trades impulsively due to FOMO (Fear of Missing Out).

- **Set Realistic Goals:** Avoid setting unrealistic profit expectations. Aim for consistent, steady growth rather than quick gains.

- **Mindfulness and Meditation:** Practice mindfulness and meditation techniques to stay present and reduce stress.

These practices enhance emotional control and decision-making.

- **Take Breaks:** Step away from the screen regularly to refresh your mind. Overtrading can lead to emotional fatigue and poor decision-making.

- **Keep a Trading Journal:** Document your trades, emotions, and thought processes. Reviewing your journal can help identify patterns and improve your decision-making over time.

- **Limit Screen Time:** Avoid obsessively watching price movements. Excessive screen time can lead to impulsive trading and heightened emotions.

- **Positive Self-Talk:** Cultivate a positive inner dialogue. Replace negative self-talk with constructive and rational thoughts.

- **Avoid Revenge Trading:** After a loss, take time to analyze what went wrong before placing another trade. Avoid chasing losses out of frustration.

- **Stay Flexible:** Markets can be unpredictable. Be prepared to adapt your strategies based on changing market conditions.

- **Seek Support:** Connect with other traders, mentors, or professionals. Discussing your challenges and seeking advice can provide valuable insights and emotional support.

- **Visualization:** Visualize successful trades and your trading plan being executed. Visualization can help you maintain a focused and confident mindset.

- **Celebrate Small Wins:** Acknowledge and celebrate your achievements, even if they are small. Positive reinforcement can boost your confidence and motivation.

- **Understand Losses are Part of Trading:** Accept that losses are inevitable in trading. Avoid dwelling on losses and instead focus on learning from them.

- Remember that emotional mastery takes time and practice. Emotions will always be present, but with consistent effort and the implementation of effective strategies, you can learn to manage them and make decisions that are more objective in your trading journey.

- **Dealing with Emotions While Trading: Harnessing the Power of Self-Awareness**

- The world of trading in financial markets is a high-stakes, dynamic arena where emotions often run high. Managing these emotions effectively is essential for making informed decisions and maintaining a rational, disciplined approach. Self-awareness is a foundational element in the toolkit of every successful trader, enabling them to recognize and acknowledge their emotional responses and understand how feelings such as fear, greed, excitement, and frustration can significantly impact their decision-making.

1. Recognition of Emotions:

The first step in dealing with emotions while trading is to recognize their presence. Emotions are an intrinsic part of human nature, and they are bound to surface when trading, especially in moments of uncertainty or volatility. By being attuned to your emotional state, you can begin to gain control over how these feelings influence your trading decisions.

2. Understanding Fear:

Fear is a potent and often paralyzing emotion in the world of trading. It can manifest when a trade is going against your expectations or when there is a significant potential for loss. Recognizing fear is crucial, as it can prompt impulsive actions like closing a trade prematurely or avoiding viable opportunities. Understanding that fear is a natural response to risk is the first step in preventing it from driving hasty decisions.

3. Navigating Greed:

Greed, the desire for excessive gains, can also be a detrimental force in trading. It can lead to overtrading, taking on too much risk, or refusing to lock in profits when the time is right. Recognizing when greed is influencing your decisions is essential for maintaining a balanced and disciplined trading strategy. Consider that trading is a marathon, not a sprint, and maintaining consistent, moderate gains is often more sustainable than chasing extraordinary returns.

4. Handling Excitement:

Excitement can result from a successful trade or a sudden market movement in your favor. While excitement is a positive emotion, it can also cloud judgment and lead to impulsive decisions. Recognize that excitement should not drive your trading strategy; instead, rely on your well-researched plans and risk management techniques to make informed choices.

5. Tackling Frustration:

Frustration is a common emotional response when things aren't going your way in trading. It can lead to revenge trading, where you try to recoup losses by taking high-risk positions. Understanding that frustration can exacerbate losses and that it's essential to take a step back, reevaluate your strategy, and maintain discipline in challenging times is critical.

6. Developing Emotional Discipline:

Self-awareness is the foundation, but emotional discipline is the building block that follows. Once you recognize and understand how emotions can impact your trading, you can work on developing strategies to manage them effectively. This might involve setting clear entry and exit points, implementing stop-loss orders, or even taking breaks from trading during highly emotional periods.

7. Keeping a Trading Journal:

Maintaining a trading journal is a valuable tool for tracking and analyzing your emotions during trades. Record not only the technical aspects of your trades but also your emotional state at different points. This can help you identify patterns and triggers that lead to emotional responses and create strategies to counteract them.

Dealing with Emotions While Trading: The Power of Education

Trading in financial markets is a multifaceted endeavor that often challenges traders on both technical and emotional fronts. As emotions can significantly impact trading decisions, it is crucial to harness the power of education to mitigate their influence. By learning about trading strategies, market dynamics, and risk management, traders empower themselves to make more informed decisions and reduce the emotional reactions that can lead to impulsive, less rational choices.

1. Trading Strategies:

Education in trading strategies provides traders with a solid foundation for navigating the complexities of financial markets. Understanding the principles and nuances of different trading approaches, such as day trading, swing trading, or long-term investing, helps traders develop a structured plan that aligns with their goals and risk tolerance. This knowledge not only provides a clear roadmap for trading but also instills confidence, reducing the anxiety and uncertainty often associated with emotional decision-making.

2. Market Dynamics:

Learning about market dynamics is akin to studying the language of financial markets. It involves gaining insights into how supply and demand forces interact, the impact of economic indicators, and the influence of geopolitical events. Understanding these dynamics enables traders to interpret price movements and recognize potential trading opportunities based on concrete market conditions. By reducing uncertainty, education in market dynamics helps traders make decisions rooted in analysis rather than emotional reactions.

3. Risk Management:

One of the most critical aspects of trading education is acquiring knowledge about risk management. This entails understanding how to protect capital, minimize potential losses, and determine appropriate position sizes. By grasping the principles of risk management, traders can establish predefined stop-loss levels, manage leverage effectively, and allocate their capital prudently. This not only reduces the emotional stress associated with trading but also safeguards against catastrophic losses.

4. Technical Analysis:

Technical analysis is a vital component of trading education that equips traders with tools to analyze price charts, identify trends, and make data-driven decisions. By learning about technical indicators, chart patterns, and candlestick formations, traders can formulate strategies based on objective evidence rather than emotional intuition. This knowledge enhances the precision of trading decisions and reduces reliance on emotional responses.

5. Fundamental Analysis:

Education in fundamental analysis is another pillar of trading knowledge. It involves studying economic factors, company financials, and geopolitical developments that can impact asset prices. By understanding the fundamental drivers of market movements, traders can make informed decisions and avoid emotional reactions driven solely by headlines or market sentiment.

6. Continuous Learning:

Trading education is not a one-time endeavor but a continuous process. The dynamic nature of financial markets requires traders to stay informed about emerging trends, new strategies, and evolving market dynamics. Ongoing learning not only deepens a trader's knowledge but also enhances adaptability, reducing the anxiety associated with uncertainty.

7. Backtesting and Simulation:

Education can also encompass the practice of backtesting and trading simulations. By historically testing trading strategies and practicing with virtual portfolios, traders gain hands-on experience without the risk of real capital. This helps build confidence and emotional resilience by allowing traders to encounter and learn from challenges in a controlled environment.

Dealing with Emotions While Trading: The Blueprint of a Trading Plan

Trading in financial markets is an arena where emotions can run high and disrupt rational decision-making. The trading plan, a meticulously crafted document that encompasses entry and exit criteria, risk management rules, and contingencies for various scenarios, serves as the ultimate antidote to emotional trading.

By adhering to a well-structured plan, traders can significantly reduce the influence of their emotions and maintain a disciplined and methodical approach to trading.

1. Entry and Exit Criteria:

A robust trading plan provides clear, objective guidelines for entering and exiting trades. These criteria are based on technical and fundamental analysis, leaving little room for emotional decision-making. Entry criteria specify the conditions under which a trade should be initiated, such as specific price levels, technical indicators, or fundamental factors aligning in a particular way. Exit criteria define the conditions for closing a trade, whether it's hitting a predetermined profit target or a stop-loss level to limit losses. By following these criteria, traders can avoid impulsive decisions driven by emotions like fear or greed.

2. Risk Management Rules:

Effective risk management is at the heart of a solid trading plan. It encompasses setting the maximum amount of capital to risk in a single trade, defining position sizes, and establishing stop-loss orders. Risk management rules are designed to safeguard a trader's capital, ensuring that no single trade can result in catastrophic losses. This systematic approach mitigates emotional reactions stemming from fear of substantial losses and provides peace of mind.

3. Contingencies for Different Scenarios:

The financial markets are unpredictable, and traders often encounter unexpected events. A well-thought-out trading plan includes contingencies for various scenarios. For instance, it may specify how to adjust the trading strategy if market conditions change, or what actions to take in the event of news that impacts the chosen assets. These contingencies remove the uncertainty surrounding unexpected events, reducing anxiety and emotional reactions.

4. Structured Decision-Making:

Following a trading plan fosters structured decision-making. It promotes a logical and consistent approach to trading, eliminating the emotional reactions that can lead to erratic behavior. This structured approach encourages traders to stick to their predetermined strategies, even when faced with market turbulence or the allure of quick profits.

5. Accountability and Review:

A trading plan also incorporates a mechanism for accountability and regular review. Traders can assess their performance against the plan, making necessary adjustments as they gain experience or as market conditions evolve. This continuous review process encourages self-reflection, enhances trading skills, and reduces emotional trading by reinforcing discipline.

6. Psychological Support:

Besides its technical aspects, a trading plan also serves as a psychological support system. It acts as a safety net, helping traders remain calm and focused, even in the face of losses or market volatility. Knowing that they are following a pre-established plan can alleviate the emotional stress often associated with trading.

Dealing with Emotions While Trading: The Art of Position Sizing

In the world of financial markets, where emotions often ride the rollercoaster of price fluctuations, one of the most effective strategies for maintaining a rational and disciplined approach is the art of position sizing. Position sizing involves determining the appropriate size of a trade based on your risk tolerance and the predetermined stop-loss level. By mastering this aspect of trading, you can avoid the common pitfall of risking too much of your capital on a single trade, which can be a significant source of emotional distress.

1. Risk Tolerance and Capital Preservation:

Position sizing begins with a careful assessment of your risk tolerance. Understanding how much you are willing to risk on a single trade is a fundamental aspect of risk management. It allows you to align your trading strategy with your financial goals while preserving your capital. By determining a comfortable level of risk, you can navigate the markets without being overly influenced by emotional responses to market fluctuations.

2. Stop-Loss Levels:

In conjunction with risk tolerance, position sizing relies on the establishment of clear stop-loss levels. These levels represent the point at which you are willing to exit a trade to limit potential losses. Stop-loss orders are essential for risk management and should be placed based on technical analysis, support and resistance levels, or other predefined criteria. By adhering to these levels, traders can prevent emotions like hope or fear from influencing their trading decisions.

3. Capital Allocation:

Once you've identified your risk tolerance and set stop-loss levels, you can calculate the appropriate position size. This calculation considers the distance between the entry price and the stop-loss level. The larger the potential loss (the difference between entry and stop-loss), the smaller the position size should be to align with your risk tolerance.

4. Diversification:

Position sizing also allows for effective diversification of your portfolio. By appropriately sizing positions across different assets or trades, you can spread risk and reduce the impact of a single trade on your overall portfolio. Diversification helps protect your capital and mitigate the emotional turmoil that can accompany significant losses.

5. Emotion Management:

Emotions like fear, greed, and anxiety often stem from the fear of losing a significant portion of your capital on a single trade. By sizing your positions appropriately and adhering to predetermined stop-loss levels, you gain a sense of control and discipline. This not only helps manage these emotions but also instills confidence in your trading strategy.

6. Flexibility and Adaptability:

Position sizing is a flexible strategy that can be adjusted to accommodate changing market conditions and fluctuations in risk tolerance. By continually assessing and adapting your position sizes, you can maintain a balanced and rational approach to trading, even in the face of evolving emotional challenges.

7. Consistency and Discipline:

Position sizing enforces consistency and discipline in your trading strategy. Following a systematic approach based on risk tolerance and stop-loss levels eliminates the need for impulsive or emotional decision-making. It ensures that you remain true to your trading plan and minimize the emotional rollercoaster that can plague undisciplined traders.

Dealing with Emotions While Trading: The Benefits of Taking Breaks

Trading in the fast-paced and high-pressure environment of financial markets can be emotionally taxing. Dealing with the psychological challenges that come with trading is a vital aspect of achieving long-term success. Taking breaks is a valuable strategy for managing emotions and maintaining a clear and disciplined mindset. It's a practice that helps traders refresh their minds and prevent emotional fatigue, which can lead to poor decision-making.

1. Preventing Emotional Fatigue:

Emotional fatigue is a common challenge for traders, particularly when they are exposed to continuous market fluctuations and information overload. This fatigue can manifest as heightened stress, anxiety, frustration, or impatience, all of which can compromise a trader's ability to make rational decisions. By taking breaks, traders can recharge their emotional resilience and reduce the impact of emotional fatigue.

2. Regaining Perspective:

Trading involves making decisions that have financial consequences, and these decisions can be emotionally charged. Taking a step back from the screen allows traders to regain perspective. It enables them to see the bigger picture and reevaluate their strategies without being influenced by the short-term emotional reactions that can result from constantly monitoring market movements.

3. Reducing Impulsivity:

Emotional reactions often lead to impulsive trading decisions.

Fear of missing out (FOMO) or the desire to recover losses quickly can drive impulsive actions that result in poor outcomes. Regular breaks serve as a circuit breaker for impulsive behavior. They provide traders with the opportunity to pause, reflect, and return to the trading desk with a calmer and more deliberate mindset.

4. Enhanced Focus and Concentration:

Trading requires a high degree of focus and concentration. Continuous exposure to screens and market data can lead to mental exhaustion, reducing a trader's ability to make sound decisions. Taking breaks allows the mind to recharge and enhances cognitive functions, resulting in improved focus and concentration when returning to trading activities.

5. Improved Decision-Making:

Sound decision-making is a cornerstone of successful trading. Emotions can cloud judgment and lead to irrational choices. By taking breaks, traders can regain emotional balance and make more thoughtful, well-reasoned decisions based on analysis and strategy rather than impulsive reactions to market movements.

6. Stress Reduction:

Stress is a common emotional response in trading, and excessive stress can have detrimental effects on both mental and physical well-being. Regular breaks provide a chance to reduce stress levels, which, in turn, promotes a healthier emotional state. Stress reduction can lead to a more stable and disciplined approach to trading.

7. Maintaining Work-Life Balance:

Overtrading or excessive screen time can encroach on a trader's personal life, leading to burnout and further emotional challenges. Taking breaks not only refreshes the mind but also helps maintain a healthy work-life balance, which is essential for long-term trading success.

Dealing with Emotions While Trading: The Virtue of Patience

In the fast-paced world of financial markets, emotions can often lead to impulsive actions, causing traders to make hasty decisions they later regret. One of the most valuable tools for managing emotions in trading is practicing patience. Waiting for valid trade setups that align with your strategy and avoiding the lure of impulsive trades driven by FOMO (Fear of Missing Out) is a cornerstone of disciplined trading. Here's why patience is so important in dealing with emotions while trading:

1. Eliminating Impulsive Behavior:

Impulsivity can be the root cause of emotional trading. The fear of missing out on a potentially profitable trade can lead to impulsive actions that do not align with your trading strategy. Patience, on the other hand, helps you resist the temptation to jump into trades without proper analysis and preparation. It encourages a calm and deliberate approach to decision-making.

2. FOMO Mitigation:

FOMO, or the fear of missing out, is a powerful emotional trigger in trading. Traders often succumb to FOMO by entering trades late, chasing trends, or deviating from their strategy. Practicing patience by waiting for valid trade setups helps mitigate the impact of FOMO. It allows you to resist the emotional pull of jumping into a trade simply because others are doing so.

3. Enhancing Strategy Adherence:

Patience is a key factor in adhering to your trading strategy. A well-defined strategy often includes specific criteria for trade entry and exit. By patiently waiting for these criteria to be met, you maintain consistency in your trading approach. This adherence to your strategy reduces emotional decisions that can lead to erratic trading behavior.

4. Reducing Emotional Stress:

Emotional trading can be stressful and exhausting. Impulsive trades, especially those driven by FOMO, can result in losses and emotional turmoil. By practicing patience and waiting for valid trade setups, you reduce the emotional stress associated with trading. This results in a more composed and less anxiety-ridden trading experience.

5. Enhancing Analysis:

Patience allows you to engage in thorough analysis and due diligence before entering a trade. It gives you the time to evaluate market conditions, technical and fundamental factors, and risk-reward ratios. This comprehensive analysis leads to more informed decisions and minimizes emotional guesswork.

6. Better Risk Management:

By exercising patience, you can more effectively implement risk management techniques. Waiting for the right trade setups enables you to set appropriate stop-loss levels and position sizes. This, in turn, safeguards your capital and reduces the emotional burden associated with significant losses.

7. Long-Term Sustainability:

Patience is not just a short-term virtue; it's essential for the long-term sustainability of a trading career. Impulsive trading can lead to significant losses that may be challenging to recover from. By waiting for valid trade setups, you create a sustainable trading approach that can withstand the emotional ups and downs of financial markets.

Dealing with Emotions While Trading: The Peril of Revenge Trading

In the complex world of financial markets, traders are not immune to experiencing losses. The emotional response to losses can be intense and may lead to impulsive and unwise decisions. One such emotionally driven behavior is revenge trading, where traders impulsively place trades in an attempt to recoup losses. Avoiding revenge trading is essential for maintaining discipline and making sound trading decisions. Here's why refraining from revenge trading is critical in dealing with emotions while trading:

1. Emotional Analysis:

After a loss, it's crucial to take time for emotional self-reflection and analysis. Revenge trading typically occurs when emotions like frustration, anger, or disappointment are at their peak. By avoiding revenge trading, you allow yourself the opportunity to understand the emotional factors that contributed to the loss. This self-awareness is vital for long-term improvement.

2. Objective Evaluation:

Taking a step back from trading after a loss allows you to objectively evaluate what went wrong. It helps you identify the specific reasons for the loss, whether it was a result of poor analysis, impulsive decisions, or market conditions. This objective evaluation is valuable for making necessary adjustments to your trading strategy.

3. Avoiding Impulsive Actions:

Revenge trading is often characterized by impulsive, emotional decisions. By refraining from immediate trading after a loss, you give yourself the time and space to regain emotional balance. This helps you avoid making rash decisions driven by the desire to recover losses quickly, decisions that often result in even more significant losses.

4. Reducing Emotional Stress:

Trading is a high-stress activity, and losses can be emotionally challenging. Engaging in revenge trading can intensify this emotional stress, leading to a cycle of frustration and anxiety. Avoiding revenge trading helps break this cycle and reduces the emotional burden associated with trading.

5. Enhancing Learning:

Avoiding revenge trading is essential for turning losses into valuable learning experiences. When you take the time to analyze what went wrong and make necessary adjustments, you can transform losses into opportunities for growth. This learning process can ultimately improve your trading skills and decision-making.

6. Protecting Capital:

Revenge trading often leads to an increased risk of significant losses. By avoiding impulsive actions, you protect your capital and reduce the chances of further financial setbacks. This capital preservation is crucial for the long-term sustainability of your trading career.

7. Maintaining Discipline:

Discipline is a cornerstone of successful trading. Avoiding revenge trading reinforces discipline by ensuring that your trading decisions are based on analysis, strategy, and adherence to your trading plan. This discipline reduces the likelihood of emotional and erratic trading behavior.

FINAL THOUGHTS ON SMART MONEY TRADING

As we conclude this journey through the intricacies of smart money concepts, it's important to reflect on the profound insights gained and the implications they hold for the world of trading. Smart money, often shrouded in mystery, has revealed itself as a force that shapes markets, challenges conventions, and presents opportunities for those who dare to decipher its subtle language.

In understanding the strategies of institutional players, seasoned investors, and those privy to market nuances, we've unraveled a narrative that extends beyond price charts and economic indicators. Smart money encapsulates the art of contrarian thinking, the poise of calculated risk-taking, and the dynamic interplay between informed decision-making and market sentiment.

The journey has illuminated the transformative power of knowledge. Armed with insights into how smart money moves, traders possess a compass guiding them through the intricate maze of market fluctuations. Yet, this enlightenment comes with a responsibility – to practice sound risk management, adhere to disciplined strategies, and temper the allure of impulse with the wisdom of informed analysis.

In a landscape that often celebrates instant gratification, the smart money concept reminds us of the virtue of patience. It encourages us to see beyond the noise, to navigate beyond the trends, and to uncover the threads of opportunity woven into the fabric of the markets.

As you move forward armed with these insights, remember that the world of trading is as much about adaptability as it is about technique. Smart money, while a beacon of guidance, is also a testament to the ever-evolving nature of financial markets. Flexibility and continuous learning are the currencies that can keep you in tune with the rhythm of market dynamics.

And so, with newfound knowledge and a deepened appreciation for the art and science of trading, we bid adieu to this exploration of smart money concepts. May your trading journey be enriched by the wisdom acquired here, and may you navigate the markets with the finesse and acumen befitting those who decipher the language of the masters of capital.   --------Safe travels on your trading odyssey,------

BUY ME A COFFEE

https://www.buymeacoffee.com/cynaut

COMMON MISTAKES
WHEN TRADING

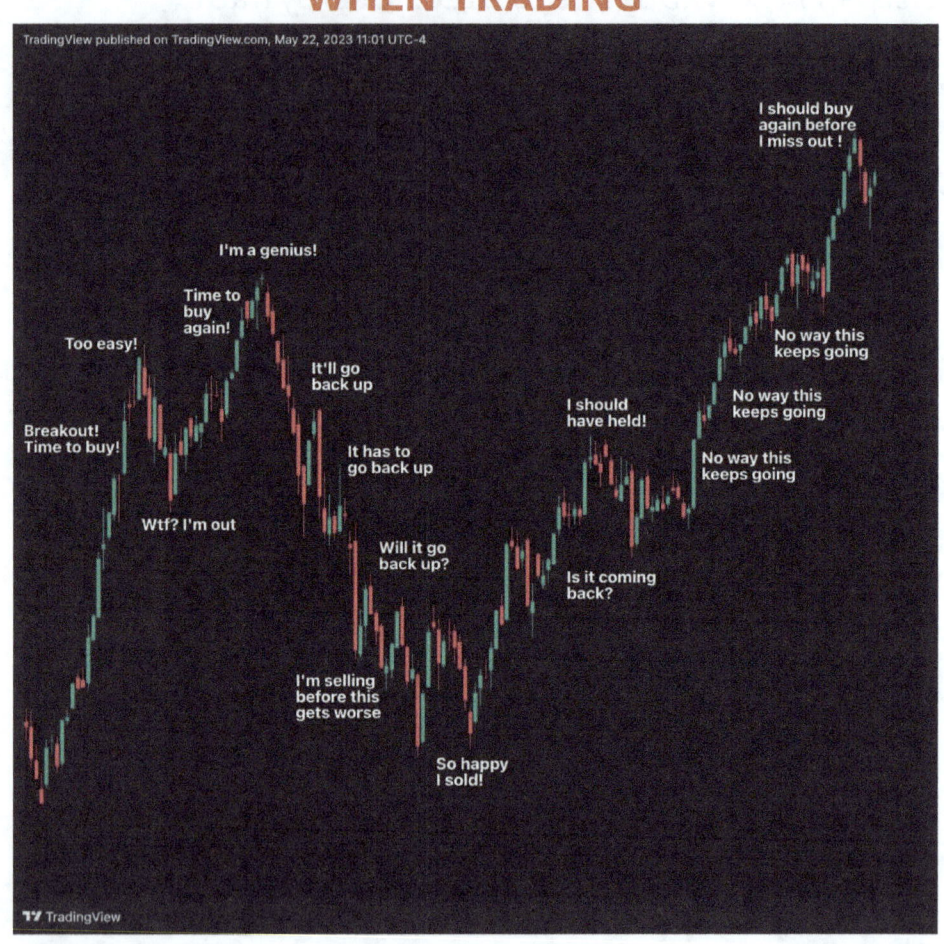

"IF YOUR JOB IS YOUR ONLY SOURCE

OF INCOME YOU ARE ONE STEP AWAY FROM POVERTY"

**OPEN YOUR FOREX ACCOUNT
NOW WITH THE BEST BROKERS
<u>USE THE LINKS BELOW</u>**

DERIV BROKER: https://
bit.ly/41z2CJo

EXNESS BROKER: https://
one.exnesstrack.com/
a/h652oo8773

©2023 LENTLE ANDRIAS

WhatsApp No. +267 73 105 698

Email: lentleandrias@gmail.com

BUY ME A COFFEE

https://www.buymeacoffee.com/cynaut

BITCOIN

1HExG9zdjyLDb4H7hPTapvLbrc9gn8Jt1v

www.ingramcontent.com/pod-product-compliance
Lightning Source LLC
Chambersburg PA
CBHW072329290526
45794CB00002B/796